THIS BOOK IS DEDICATED TO MY DELIGHTFUL NIECES AND NEPHEW.
JUST WHEN YOU THOUGHT YOUR UNCLE COULDN'T GET ANY STRANGER, HERE'S ANOTHER
ADVENTURE TO BAMBOOZLE YOU AGAIN. GET READY FOR EVEN MORE CURIOUS
ESCAPADES AND SURPRISES THAT WILL KEEP YOU GUESSING.

MUCH LOVE,
FUNKLE MIKE.
(FUN UNCLE)

PEA PEA

NEEDS A WIPE

Chapter 1

I HAD AN ACCIDENT EARLIER WITH A VERY JUICY APPLE.
I DON'T LIKE BEING COVERED IN APPLESAUCE.

REMINDING WEE WEE NOT TO EAT ME OR CHI CHI HAS BEEN RATHER DIFFICULT.

WE ARE RUNNING LOW ON APPLE. WE SHOULD PROBABLY GET TO THE VILLAGE SOON.

THERE ARE TINY BEETLES FOLLOWING US.
THEY'RE LICKING THEIR LIPS JUST LIKE WEE WEE DOES.

ARE THESE YOUR FRIENDS WEE WEE? THEY ARE PROBABLY WONDERING HOW YOU GOT SO BIG!

HELLO LITTLE WEEVIL AND RHINO BEETLE!
HOW ARE YOU TODAY?

I'M PEA PEA AND THIS IS CHI CHI.
PLEASE DON'T EAT US.

WE CAN'T FORGET WEE WEE!
DON'T EAT WEE WEE EITHER. RIGHT WEE WEE?

IF YOU EAT ME, THEN I HAVE TO TAKE YOU TO THE FABRIC OF TIME. UNFORTUNATELY, I'M TOO BUSY TRYING TO GET CLEANED UP.

DON'T WORRY ABOUT BEING EATEN.
THEY'RE RUNNING AWAY, PEA PEA! I DON'T
THINK THEY UNDERSTAND US.

IF ONLY I COULD SPEAK THE BEAUTIFUL LANGUAGE OF THE WEEVILS.

WE SHOULD GO FIND DEW DEW. I'M THIRSTY AND YOU CAN FINALLY CLEAN UP, PEA PEA!

GOOD IDEA CHI CHI! WEE WEE, YOU LIKE WATER, RIGHT?
EARLY MORNING IS THE BEST TIME TO VISIT DEW DEW'S STORE.

Chapter 2

DO YOU THINK I WAS FRIENDLY ENOUGH TO THOSE WEEVILS?

I FEEL BAD FOR NOT INVITING THEM ALONG.

IT'S OK WEE WEE! DEW DEW IS A FRIENDLY GARDEN SPIDER. RIGHT, DEW DEW?

GOOD MORNING! I'M DEBBIE DEW DEW AND IT'S A PLEASURE TO MEET YOU.

NOW I UNDERSTAND WHY THOSE OTHER BEETLES STOPPED FOLLOWING US. THEY'RE SCARED OF SPIDERS.

LOOK, WEE WEE! EVERYTHING IS FINE! DEW DEW AND I HAVE BEEN FRIENDS FOR A LONG WHILE.

HAVE YOU ALSO BEEN TO THE FABRIC OF TIME, WEE WEE? PRETTY GREAT, RIGHT?

SEE, WEE WEE? NOTHING TO WORRY ABOUT.

I DON'T KNOW WHY I EVER TRIED TO EAT PEA PEA. HE'S GREAT!

YOU NEED A SHOWER, MY FRIEND.
STAND AT THE END OF MY WEB FOR ME.

LET'S DRY YOU OFF WITH A TOWEL.
THE CLOTH IS NICE, RIGHT? I FIND ALL SORTS
OF TORN UP PIECES AT THE FARM.

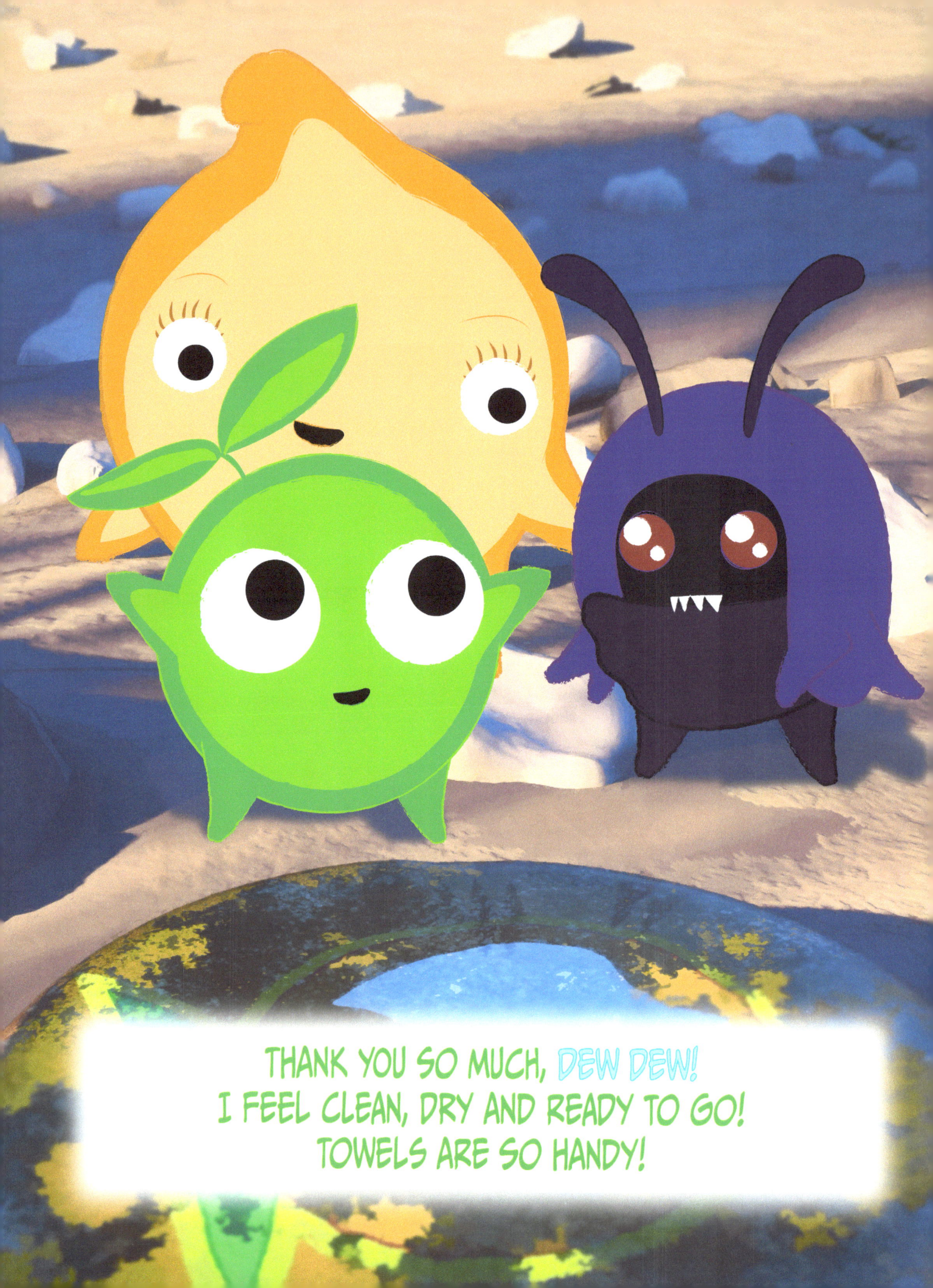

THANK YOU SO MUCH, DEW DEW!
I FEEL CLEAN, DRY AND READY TO GO!
TOWELS ARE SO HANDY!

Chapter 3

DOES ANYONE NEED ANYTHING BEFORE
WE GET GOING? I'M PRETTY EXCITED
TO TRY PANTS ON.

MAY WE GET THREE WRAPPED
DEW DROPS FOR OUR TRAVELS?

NOW, DON'T BLINK AS I WRAP THIS OK?

YOU PROBABLY BLINKED.

I WAS CERTAIN THAT I DIDN'T BLINK, BUT HERE WE ARE!

WHAT DO YOU THINK OF CLOTHES, DEW DEW?

I'VE TRIED ON BOOTS. THEY LOOKED GREAT, BUT I COULDN'T CLIMB ANYTHING. I WOULD LOVE A HAT!

LET'S GO TO RA-TAH-TAT AND PICK UP A HAT FOR DEW DEW!
WE CAN TRY ON A LOT OF FUN CLOTHES THERE TOO!

YOU WOULD DO THAT FOR ME?
WELL THEN, ALLOW ME TO GIVE
YOU THOSE DEW DROPS FOR FREE.

THAT IS VERY KIND OF YOU, DEW DEW.
WHAT A GREAT FRIEND YOU ARE!

YOU'RE A GREAT FRIEND TOO, PEA PEA. YOU HELPED CALM CAW CAW DOWN AND SHE NO LONGER TRIES TO EAT ME!

A FRIENDLY UNION OF DEW DEW AND CAW CAW?
THAT WARMS MY HEART! THANKS AGAIN FOR
EVERYTHING. SEE YOU AGAIN SOON!

MICHAEL (MIKE) CORR IS A PROFESSIONAL GRAPHIC ARTIST SPECIALIZING IN ART, ANIMATION AND VISUAL EFFECTS. HIS EXPERTISE IN 3D MODELLING AND TEXTURING IS EVIDENT IN ANIMATED SHORT FILMS INCLUDING KIMOTIWIN: THE ACT OF STEALING, MONSTR AND FREAKY TALES. HE ALSO WORKED ON TELEVISION SERIES INCLUDING THE SUMMONER, BIGFOOT AND GARY AND HIS DEMONS. MIKE AND THE TEAM AT SOLIS ANIMATION INC, RECENTLY CREATED A FULL-LENGTH FEATURE FILM, S(KIDS) WHICH PREMIERED AT ANNECY INTERNATIONAL FILM FESTIVAL IN FRANCE.

MIKE COLLABORATED ON MORE THAN 30 MUSIC VIDEOS. MIKE'S PASSION FOR CREATING VISUAL EXPERIENCES HAS EXTENDED TO WRITING AND ILLUSTRATING CHILDREN'S STORIES. HIS SECOND BOOK, PEA PEA NEEDS A WIPE (2025), IS AVAILABLE ON AMAZON.

PEA PEA (2024), THE FIRST BOOK IN THE SERIES, IS ALSO AVAILABLE ON AMAZON.

MIKE LIVES AND WORKS IN TORONTO ALONG WITH HIS DOG ROBIN.

www.ingramcontent.com/pod-product-compliance
Lightning Source LLC
LaVergne TN
LVHW072104070426

835508LV00003B/261